# WORLDfocus

# India

## AMANDA BARKER

# Contents

# Introduction

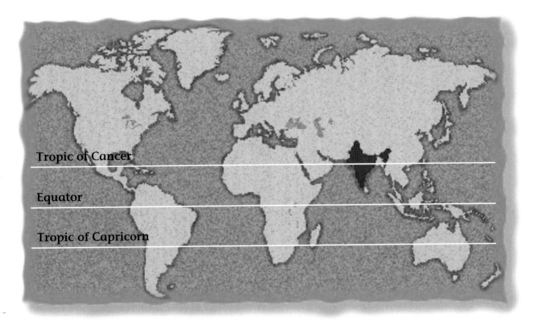

Tropic of Cancer

Equator

Tropic of Capricorn

India is a large country in Asia, with a complex history and culture. The British ruled most of India from 1849 until 1947. **Mahatma Gandhi** led a non-violent movement towards independence, and in 1947 India became a free country again. India is now the largest **democracy** in the world.

△ **Where is India?**

If you were to travel through India from north to south, you would see many changes in the landscape. The highest mountains are in the north. They are part of the Himalayan mountain range. But right next to them the south of the Himalayas is the flattest and most fertile land in India. Crops grow very well here. The River Ganges winds its way eastwards towards the Bay of Bengal. To the west is the Thar Desert.

◁ **Few plants grow on the dry sands of the Thar Desert.**

2

AFGHANISTAN

PAKISTAN

*Thar Desert*

TIBET

H i m a l a y a s

NEPAL

BHUTAN

*Brahmaputra*

*Ganges*

*Ganges*

BANGLA-
DESH

Tropic of Cancer

INDIAN
OCEAN

**INDIA**

ARABIAN
SEA

*Godavari*

BAY
OF
BENGAL

BURMA
(Myanmar)

*Deccan Plateau*

*Western Ghats*

*Krishna*

*Eastern Ghats*

**The main
features of India.**

Mountains

SRI
LANKA

0        645 km

0        400 miles

N

W        E

S

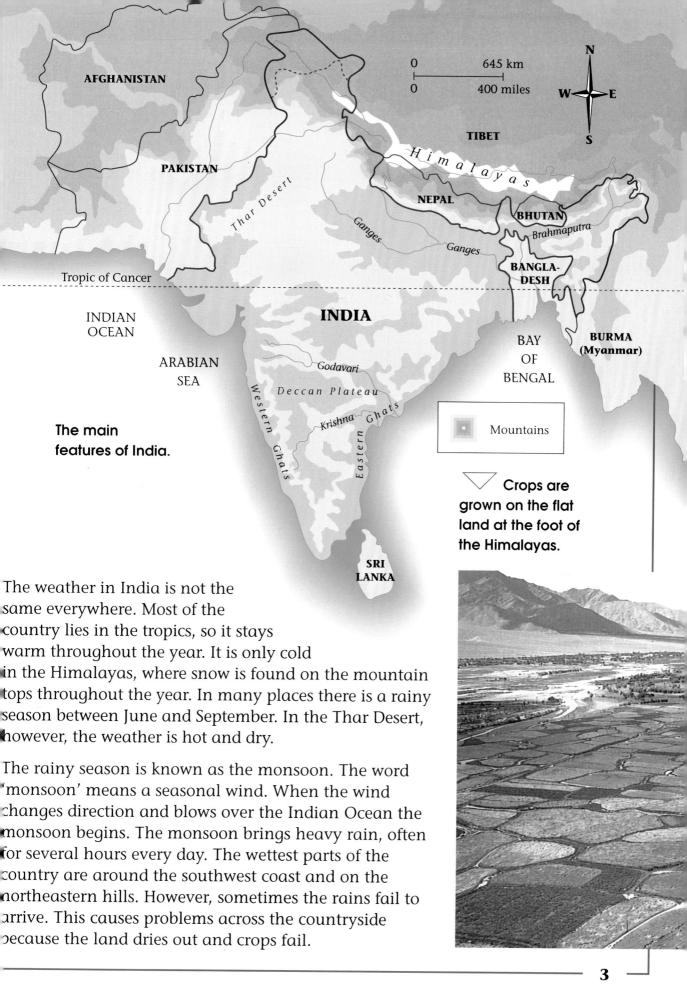

⬇ **Crops are
grown on the flat
land at the foot of
the Himalayas.**

The weather in India is not the
same everywhere. Most of the
country lies in the tropics, so it stays
warm throughout the year. It is only cold
in the Himalayas, where snow is found on the mountain
tops throughout the year. In many places there is a rainy
season between June and September. In the Thar Desert,
however, the weather is hot and dry.

The rainy season is known as the monsoon. The word
'monsoon' means a seasonal wind. When the wind
changes direction and blows over the Indian Ocean the
monsoon begins. The monsoon brings heavy rain, often
for several hours every day. The wettest parts of the
country are around the southwest coast and on the
northeastern hills. However, sometimes the rains fail to
arrive. This causes problems across the countryside
because the land dries out and crops fail.

# The people

In this vast country there are many contrasts in the way people live. There are many differences in the appearance, language, writing, customs and religions of the Indian people.

There are eighteen official languages, and hundreds of different dialects throughout India. Hindi is the most commonly used language, although only about one-fifth of the people speak it. English is the second language for many Indians. English or Hindi is often spoken when people from two different parts of the country meet. Many people speak or understand at least two languages. The Prime Minister in 1994, Narasimha Rao, speaks at least eight of the Indian languages.

Religion plays an important part in most people's lives in India. Eighty-three per cent of Indian people belong to the **Hindu** faith. Hindus believe that a person's soul is born again, after death, into another body. This rebirth is called reincarnation.

Every Hindu village in India has a temple and most people belonging to this faith have a small shrine at home where they can pray. The **caste system** is a part of the Hindu religion. Lower caste people are generally poor. Traditionally, only very high caste Hindus, called Brahmins, can be priests. The very lowest castes were known as **Untouchables**. The government in India has outlawed the idea of Untouchability.

Hindu festivals are celebrated throughout the year. The most well known is **Diwali**, the festival of light. Hindus often make a pilgrimage to the banks of the River Ganges, which they regard as a sacred river.

Although about 750 million Indians are Hindus, there are other important religions too. Just under 100 million people are **Muslims** and about 49 million people are **Buddhists**, **Sikhs**, **Jains** or **Christians**.

A Hindu wedding is a colourful and exciting event.

These Indian boys are being taught about their religion.

The Sikh and Buddhist religions began in India. In the Sikh religion only one God is worshipped and there is no caste system. Buddhists follow the teachings of the Buddha, who said that people are reincarnated until they reach a state of perfect peace, called Nirvana. There are also many Christians in India.

Indian culture, music, arts and dances are often linked to religion. The best known musical instruments are the sitar (a stringed instrument) and the tabla (a twin drum). Dances may be based on religious stories. The dancers use complicated movements of the eyes, hands and face to act out the story. Sport is also important. The Indian cricket team is one of the best in the world, and India has given the world the games of chess and polo.

# Where do people live?

India has the second largest population in the world. In 1993 there were 903,000,000 people in India. The figure will probably rise to over one billion by the year 2000.

The Indian population is growing quickly because people generally have large families, particularly if they live in the countryside. In India, when you are old you have to rely on your children to look after you. If you have a large family you can be certain you will not be left on your own in old age. Until recently many infants died, but modern medicine has reduced the infant death rate. Now, many more children survive.

If you look at the map you can see that most people live either on the flat lands of the north or around the coasts. The land is rich and fertile in these areas, and crops grow well. The **produce** feeds many people.

About three-quarters of all Indians live in the countryside. There are 650,000 villages in India. An average-sized village is home to about 1000 people. Most people who live in these villages work on the land, but some are crafts people, doctors, teachers or shopkeepers. Many farmworkers have very small plots of land, and the food they grow feeds their families.

In the cities, modern buildings house the richer people who may work in business or industry, or as doctors, lawyers or teachers. Office, factory or shop workers often live in blocks of flats built by the government. These people are not wealthy.

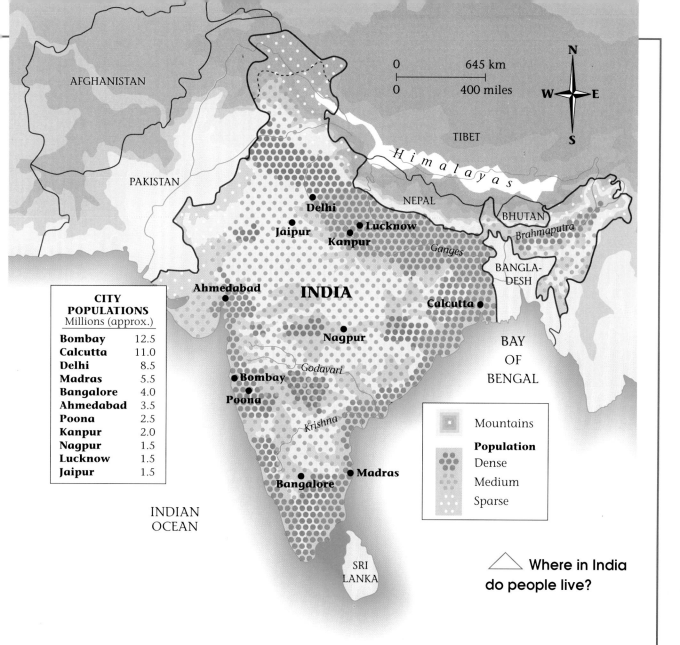

| CITY POPULATIONS Millions (approx.) | |
|---|---|
| Bombay | 12.5 |
| Calcutta | 11.0 |
| Delhi | 8.5 |
| Madras | 5.5 |
| Bangalore | 4.0 |
| Ahmedabad | 3.5 |
| Poona | 2.5 |
| Kanpur | 2.0 |
| Nagpur | 1.5 |
| Lucknow | 1.5 |
| Jaipur | 1.5 |

Where in India do people live?

Poor people often live in makeshift housing. They find it difficult to get jobs, and when they do they are often unskilled and poorly paid, like building labourers, street-cleaners or servants.

There are advantages to living in a city. There are good schools, modern hospitals and cinemas, and there are more opportunities than in the countryside. But cities can be very crowded and polluted. There may be shortages of housing, clean water and electricity because the cities are growing so fast.

**Poor people in cities may live in houses like these, without electricity or running water.**

Indian cities will continue to grow as people migrate from the countryside. They believe life will be better in the city, however it may not always turn out to be so.

# Agriculture

Today India can grow enough food to feed its people. It is self-sufficient in food. In recent years, India has donated surplus grain (rice and wheat) to famine-relief in Africa and other parts of Asia.

Well over half of the people in India work in farming. Many farmers grow food to feed their own families, and their plots of land are small. If they have any food left over they sell it at the local market. There are larger farms too, where food is mainly grown to sell for profit. About one-third of India's earnings from **exports** comes from the sale of agricultural produce.

There are also huge farms called plantations from which most of the crops are exported. Some, like cotton, may be processed by local factories. People who work on a plantation usually live there, too. They live in houses provided by the plantation owner. Children go to the plantation school and there will probably be a shop and a medical centre, too. Tea, cotton, spices, jute, tobacco, coffee and sugar are typical plantation crops grown in India.

India's farmers face many problems. Many people have to rent land and the plots are usually very small. If their crops fail they cannot pay their rent and they get into debt. Sometimes the monsoon rains fail, bringing drought and a poor harvest. The people have struggled to improve their farming methods. Money from the government and aid from overseas groups like Oxfam have helped. Many areas now have better seeds and **irrigation** systems. It is mainly the richer landowners with large farms who have been helped by these new farming methods. Many of the poorer farmers, especially those who have got into debt, have had to move to the cities because they cannot make a decent living in the country. When they leave the land, it is taken back by the landlords – so the rich farmers get even richer.

Irrigation systems channel the water to where it is needed.

△ **Paddy fields are flooded with water so that the rice plants will grow.**

Rice is the main food crop for most Indians. Wheat is grown in the cooler northern areas and millet is grown all over India. Rice farmers need plenty of water during the growing season, because rice plants will not grow unless they are standing in water. Oxfam has helped some villages to build little dams called check dams. These stop rainwater flowing away, and so help to build up underground water supplies. These supplies can then be used for crops and drinking water.

Reliable water supplies have helped, but so have the

scientific advances of the **Green Revolution**. India's farmers now produce three times as much grain as they did in 1947. More crops are grown on each farm. However, the Green Revolution has brought problems. Chemicals used to fertilize the crops and to kill weeds and pests can seep into the rivers. Water may become polluted and can poison the environment. The Green Revolution has really only worked for the larger farmers who have the money to afford the new seeds and chemicals.

# Industry

India is one of the most important industrial countries in the world. Many workers are highly skilled and the modern education system trains many young people to work in industry. India produces everything from chemicals and cars to computers. Huge power stations generate electricity. All towns and most villages have electricity.

At Independence in 1947, the Indian government realized that the country needed strong industry to develop and become wealthy. So money was invested (spent) to help industries grow.

One of the most important and successful industrial areas is the Damodar Valley west of Calcutta. Other big industrial areas have grown round large cities like Bombay and Madras.

Big industrial areas face problems. Waste from factories can cause severe water and air pollution making areas unsafe to live in. The wealth that industries create is limited. Only those people living close to the factories are likely to benefit from them. Few jobs are created when modern machinery is used to do the work. The government has also decided to spend money to help industry grow in the countryside. Small-scale projects and factories employing many people have been set up.

▽ **This man and boy are weaving cloth in a small factory.**

These workers use simple machines and tools, but use their own skills much more, for example in the hand-loom industry.

Cloth-making is a good industry to encourage. It employs many people. India grows the cotton needed and many people already have the skills needed to do this kind of work.

Indian clothes are fashionable all over the world. A lot of India's colourful cotton fabric is sold abroad. It is much better for countries such as India, which produce raw materials, to export finished goods, like clothes. Other countries will pay more for finished goods than for raw materials.

In the past, many poorer countries suffered from unfair trade. They sold their raw materials at low prices to other countries. Countries like Britain, who had bought raw materials, would turn them into finished goods. They could then charge high prices for these goods and make a lot of money. In the end, these manufacturing countries made more money than the Indians themselves, who grew the raw materials in the first place. Such unfair trading still goes on today.

Industrialization has brought a higher standard of living to many Indians. However, the benefits must be weighed against the costs. Some workers are exploited (taken advantage of) by both foreign and Indian companies who pay lower wages than they would in the USA or UK. Safety standards are often poor. In 1984 the people living in the city of Bhopal suffered from poisonous gases which escaped from an American-owned chemical factory. Thousands of people were killed, and thousands more injured – many permanently.

△ Industry is important in India, but the pollution it creates is a problem.

# Staying healthy

Poor health is linked to poverty. But what is poverty? It is being too poor to have enough to eat, and can also mean being homeless. In 1972, the **United Nations** said that about a half of India's population were living in poverty. Now only 25 per cent of people are classed as being very poor by the United Nations. Many **development agencies** say that the real figure is nearer 40 per cent, or about 360 million people.

How long you can expect to live is linked to your health, and your health is affected by how poor you are. India has improved the standard of health for many people in recent years. If you were born in India in 1960, you could expect to live for only about 44 years. Now, most people live into their sixties.

A clean water supply is very important for good health. Many diseases are transmitted (passed on) through water. If people use water which is infected by the disease cholera, for example, they can become very sick very quickly and may die. It is not hard to understand how epidemics can occur. For example, people may take their water from a river into which sewage drains. Typhoid and dysentery are also diseases which can be transmitted through water. The symptoms of each are different, but all cause fever, sickness and diarrhoea. Malaria, which is carried by mosquitoes, is also linked with water. Mosquitoes live in wet, swampy places. Malaria can cause fever and illness for many years.

▽ People like this boy can be treated quickly when accidents happen.

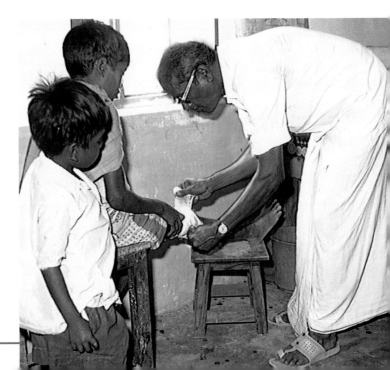

The Indian government knows how important it is to have a clean and safe water supply. To provide people with safe water, wells have been built in most villages. Now nearly 90 per cent of the population lives in a place with a clean water supply. Only 50 per cent had a clean water supply in the 1970s.

The people most at risk from illness and disease are young children. In poor countries many babies die before their first birthday from diseases like typhoid and polio. Children need a balanced diet to be strong and healthy. They also need to be protected against serious infections, like tuberculosis and polio. The number of **infant deaths** in India has halved over the last 30 years.

There are medical centres in most villages. Travelling clinics reach the most remote places. Most children are now vaccinated against serious diseases: 96 per cent against tuberculosis, and 89 per cent against diphtheria and polio.

Unfortunately, babies are still dying – mainly those born to the poorest families. Poor families may not be able to give their children a balanced diet. The children are not starving, but they are most likely to be seriously ill with measles or diarrhoea. These diseases will not kill well-fed babies, but will kill those that are weak already. The health of India's population has greatly improved, but there is still a long way to go. Health services enjoyed by the richest Indians need to be brought to the poorest in the country, too.

△ These villagers are drawing water from a well built with funds from the charity Oxfam.

# The village of Raipole

Raipole is a large village, almost like a small town, in the state of Andhra Pradesh, which is in the south of India. The maps show the location of the state and also of the village of Raipole itself.

Andhra Pradesh is roughly the same size as the UK. In 1991 there were 66 million people living there, compared to 57.5 million in the UK. On the flat land around the coast the weather is hot all year, with plenty of rain. Inland on the **plateau**, the weather is very dry for about six months (November to April). The monsoon brings the rains which usually begin in May.

Raipole is on the higher plateau land, inland from the coast. The village is home to about 2000 people. This is above the average size for an Indian village.

Most people in Raipole farm the surrounding land. Rice is the main food crop, but vegetables and spices are also grown.

▽ **The market-place in Raipole is colourful and crowded.**

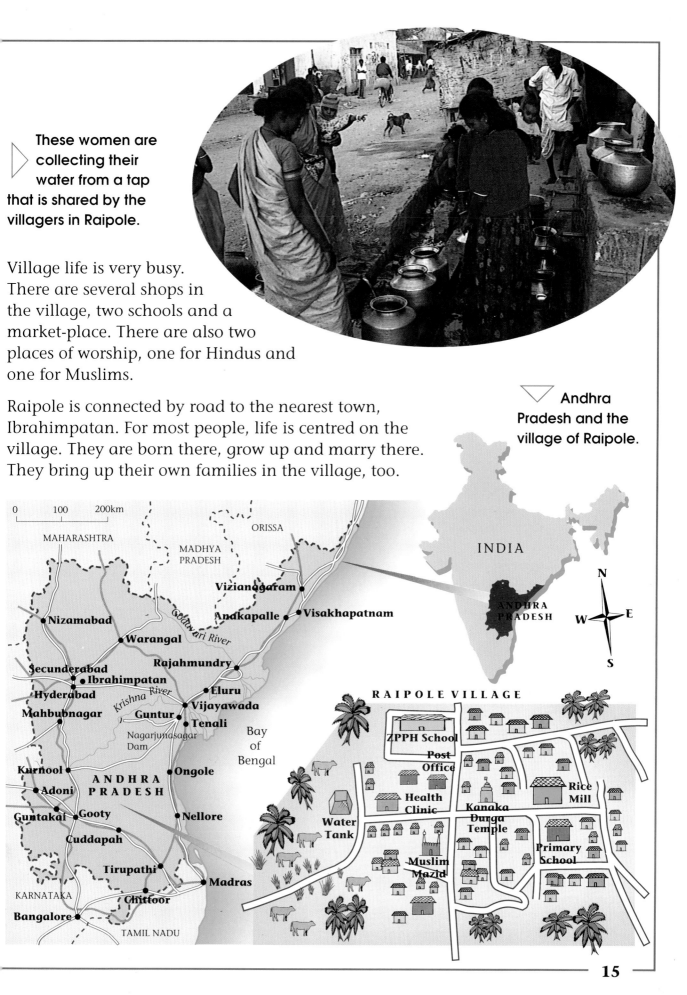

These women are collecting their water from a tap that is shared by the villagers in Raipole.

Village life is very busy. There are several shops in the village, two schools and a market-place. There are also two places of worship, one for Hindus and one for Muslims.

Raipole is connected by road to the nearest town, Ibrahimpatan. For most people, life is centred on the village. They are born there, grow up and marry there. They bring up their own families in the village, too.

Andhra Pradesh and the village of Raipole.

0    100    200km

MAHARASHTRA

ORISSA

MADHYA PRADESH

INDIA

ANDHRA PRADESH

N
W    E
S

Vizianagaram

Anakapalle    Visakhapatnam

Nizamabad

Godavari River

Warangal

Rajahmundry

Secunderabad
Ibrahimpatan
Hyderabad    Eluru
Krishna River    Vijayawada
Mahbubnagar    Guntur
Tenali
Nagarjunasagar Dam    Bay of Bengal

Kurnool    Ongole
ANDHRA PRADESH
Adoni
Guntakal    Gooty    Nellore
Cuddapah

Tirupathi    Madras

KARNATAKA    Chittoor

Bangalore

TAMIL NADU

RAIPOLE VILLAGE

ZPPH School
Post Office
Rice Mill
Health Clinic    Kanaka Durga Temple
Water Tank
Primary School
Muslim Mazid

15

# Village life

In Raipole most of the villagers work on the land. Some own their own land; others work as day-labourers for landlords. Rice is the main crop. It is often sold to make a profit, but is also grown to feed the villagers. Rice is grown on irrigated land. Water collected during the rainy season is stored in irrigation ponds, called tanks, and then channelled to the **paddy fields** when needed. There is a rice mill in the village. This is a small factory where the rice is taken out of its husks, ready to sell at the market.

About 50 families in the village are shepherds. Each keeps about 200 sheep. The sheep graze on the land surrounding the paddy fields. Shepherds make a living by selling both the wool and lambs.

▷ The wool from the sheep is spun into thread, ready to be sold.

Not everyone in the village is a farmer or shepherd. There are shopkeepers, a blacksmith (who makes and mends tools), cobblers (who make shoes and sandals and other leather goods), a vet, a doctor and several teachers. Fourteen families work as potters, making roof tiles as well as pots. There are also weavers. They make the beautiful silks used to make saris – the traditional dress of Hindu women.

▷ A shepherd takes his flock of sheep to graze in the countryside.

A job you may not have heard of is that of the **toddy tapper**. Toddy is a very popular drink made from the juice collected (or tapped) from the palm tree. More than 50 families make their living tapping toddy in Raipole.

The carpenters in the village make and mend anything from doors to ploughs to babies' cots. Washer-women make a living by doing other people's laundry. There is also a baker. Religious leaders live and work in Raipole. There is both a Muslim and a Hindu priest.

Most of the village children attend school. But they are also expected to do some of the family's work. They often help after school and during the holidays, earning much needed money for their family.

△ These women are selling their goods at the market in Raipole.

# School

△ **Children arriving at the ZPPH school in Raipole.**

In India, all children between the ages of five and fourteen can go to school. In fact, not everyone attends regularly. Children are sometimes needed to help their parents in their work. The government has made 'Education for all' one of its most important aims. In Andhra Pradesh only 56 per cent of men and 34 per cent of women can read and write. This figure will improve as the present generation of children grows up. Many of the children of today go to school, while their parents did not.

In Raipole there is a place at school for everyone. The two schools in the village are the Zilla Praja Parishad High school (ZPPH school) and a privately-owned primary school.

Most children attend the ZPPH school. This has 750 pupils in 10 classes. Children start here when they are five and most leave when they are fourteen. You will notice from the pictures that the children are all smartly dressed in a uniform.

School starts at 10 a.m. with an outdoor assembly. A boy or girl reads out the headlines from the newspaper to all the children. Next they sing the national anthem together before going to the classroom. The children study maths, social studies, general science, Hindi and English. Telugu, the local language, is also taught. Children learn about modern farming methods, and health and hygiene.

Although religion is very important to Indian culture, India is a **secular** state. This means that children do not have to study religious education in school.

The pupils have an hour off after lessons finish at 1 p.m. They all bring a packed lunch from home. The boys usually take theirs into the fields and play. The girls group together at a friend's house. After lunch, everyone goes back to school until 4 p.m. In the afternoon the boys and girls are put into separate groups to play sports and games. When they get home, they have to help their families either in the home or with their work.

▽ These children are studying their text books during a history lesson.

# Spare time

People in India work very hard. Their day is long. Many adults, especially women start work soon after dawn and only finish at dusk. People take a long lunch break in the middle of the day because it is very hot. People do manage to find some free time. They relax, and spend their time in many different ways.

Raipole is in the countryside and people have different opportunities to those living in the towns and cities. In the towns there are cinemas and restaurants. Cricket matches take place and there is always something to see and do.

The villagers of Raipole also enjoy their spare time, but in different ways. The children often play cricket after school. Adults, mainly the men meet in the evenings, after the day's work is done. In Raipole there is a tree in the market-place with a cement platform built around it. This is a very popular meeting place where the men gather to discuss the news or to talk about village life. The tea-stall is another busy meeting place where people can chat over a drink.

These children do not have stumps for the wicket, but they still enjoy a game of cricket.

Films are probably the most popular form of entertainment in India. More films are made every year in India than in any other country. The villagers of Raipole have to catch a bus to the nearest town to visit the cinema. Many people enjoy watching films on television, though most families do not have a television set. Groups of neighbours sometimes gather at a friend's house to watch their favourite programme.

Religion is an important part of everyone's life. Most people are Hindu and regularly visit the temple in the village. In many homes there is an altar so that the family can pray whenever they want to. There is also a mosque for the Muslim people in Raipole. Religious festivals are often celebrated and a wedding is a big village occasion. Most people in the village attend and a huge feast is prepared to celebrate the occasion.

Family and friends gather round the television to watch a film.

# Veerachari's day

Veerachari is ten years old and he lives with his family in Raipole. In India, families are often large and it is common for grandparents, aunts, uncles and cousins to live together. Veerachari has two sisters and a baby brother. His grandfather and his cousin also live with the family. This is a small family, by Indian standards.

The house in which Veerachari lives has five rooms. Three rooms are bedrooms, one room is a living room and the other room is the carpentry workshop. There is no bathroom or kitchen. Water has to be collected every day from a shared tap in the street. The family washes and the food is cooked outside the house in the yard. The yard is as much a part of the home as the bedrooms or living room.

△ Because Veerachari wants to become a doctor, he must study hard at school.

Veerachari goes to the ZPPH school. He is in the sixth grade and Telugu (the local language) is his favourite subject. He cycles to school every day and gives his cousin a ride.

After school, Veerachari cycles home and changes out of his uniform. He is expected to help his father in the carpentry workshop when he gets home.

Veerachari gives his cousin a ride to school on the crossbar of his bicycle.

A game of kabbadi is enjoyed after a hard day's work.

Neither of his parents went to school, but his father is a skilled carpenter. He learned his skill from his father, as most of his generation did. When Veerachari leaves school he does not want to become a carpenter. He hopes to go to university instead and learn to be a doctor.

Veerachari usually has time to play with his friends in the village before his evening meal and bedtime. His favourite game is kabbadi. This is a kind of tag. There are two teams. One team tries to run from one side of the pitch to the other. The second team has to stop them.

As soon as he gets home from school, Veerachari helps his father with the carpentry.

# Travelling around Raipole

In Andhra Pradesh transport networks are not so well developed as in some other parts of the country. Only about 43 per cent of all the villages are connected by all-weather tarred roads. There are only about eighteen cars to every thousand people in the state. Bicycles and carts are far more common.

The pictures of the village show that the roads in and around Raipole are just dirt tracks. These are fine for most of the year, but it is very difficult to use motor vehicles on them during the rainy season when the tracks turn to mud.

Most people travel around on foot during the day. The distances to work and school are no more than about 2 kilometres. No one commutes to town every day. Most families own a bicycle and short distances can be travelled quickly.

▽ **Villagers squeeze aboard a truck ready to set off for a wedding.**

△ Oxen pulling a heavy load is a common sight in India.

Heavy loads like paddy rice or castor seeds are carried from the fields to market in a cart pulled by oxen.

For the people of Raipole the bus is the main method of transport for longer distances. The village does not have a railway line nearby. The bus stop is in the centre of the village and buses run regularly through the day to Ibrahimpatan. Buses are cheap to use and are owned by the government.

A less common type of transport is a tractor or truck. These are useful when a large group of people wish to travel together. For example, the photograph opposite shows villagers on a truck. They are all going to a wedding in the next village. Tractors and trucks are hired out, and as many people as possible squeeze on to share the cost.

# Journeys

Although about three-quarters of India's population live in the countryside, 232,500,000 people live in the towns and cities (almost the same number of people as the entire population of the USA). By the year 2000, there will probably be more than 300 million living in the cities and towns.

Every year, many people leave the countryside to live in the nearest town or city. They must make a journey across the country by bus, rail or even air. Town-folk also travel to visit their relatives in their home villages.

Some people may **emigrate** to places like Canada or the Gulf States. In the 1960s many Indians went to live in the UK, too. To visit relatives abroad Indians may choose to travel by air. *Air India* is the Indian airline company that flies to most of the world's largest countries. *Indian Airlines* operates within the country. However, travel by air is expensive and only richer people can afford the fares.

▽ This man is running to catch his bus, as it arrives in a small town.

India is famous for its railways. It has the fourth largest rail network in the world. There are 60,000 kilometres of track. Every day 11 million passengers travel by train. Most of the older railway lines were built by the British in the 19th century. Since then, India has updated some of its lines and introduced diesel and electric trains in places. But you may still see steam locomotives working today, and some tourists come specially to India to 'train spot'. Locomotives driven by steam are used because there is plenty of coal in India to fire them.

△ **Travellers arrive and prepare to leave at New Delhi railway station**

People who leave the countryside to live in the towns usually travel by train. Most small towns and large villages are connected to the rail network. Passengers can carry most of their belongings on trains.

Bus and railway routes are closely linked. All railway stations are on a bus route and people can go anywhere by bus. India's main roads are fairly good and it is sometimes quicker to travel by bus than by train. Many of the buses are comfortable, and some have videos. Only the richest people have their own cars in India. There are about two cars to every thousand people in India compared to about four hundred to every thousand people in the developed world.

# Looking at India

India

▷ Indian food is popular all over the world.

△ India's cricketers in action.

India today is a mixture of old and new, with both ancient and modern ways of life. Many of the people's lives and living standards are similar to those in Western countries. But of course, there are many poor people, too.

We have many images of a country in our minds, even if we have never actually visited the place. One of the main aims of this book is to encourage you to realize that India is a huge and varied country. Although there is great poverty in India, there is also great richness of culture. The photographs in this book show some of the aspects of India.

India is a country with many natural riches. Its landscape is beautiful. There are useful natural resources to be found in the rocks and the soil. There are many famous temples and monuments, like the Taj Mahal.

The people of India have faced many struggles since 1947, when the country became independent from the British rule. The ever-growing population has needed more food, more jobs and more housing, year after year. Foreign countries have helped, by giving loans, grants and advice to help the country develop. Charities like Oxfam have also given their assistance. However, it has been the people of India themselves who have improved their own lives by sheer hard work and determination. By reading this book you will have gained an insight into the lives of Indian people today.

▽ The Taj Mahal.

▷ A colourful display of saris in a market.

# Glossary

**Buddhism** This religion began in India in 500 B.C. and has spread all over the world. Buddhists teach that all life is suffering, but through re-birth Nirvana will be reached.

**Caste System** A type of class system linked to the Hindu religion. Caste is decided by birth, it cannot be changed. People born into a high caste are allowed to do the best jobs, the lower castes get the dirtiest and most poorly paid jobs.

**Christian** Christians believe in Jesus as the son of God and read the Holy Bible.

**Democracy** A Democratic country has a government which has been freely elected by the people. Adults vote at an election for the Government of their choice.

**Development Agency** A group or organization set up to improve living conditions for people living in poorer countries. Sometimes charities fund such groups and governments may also contribute money to pay for Development Agencies.

**Diwali** The happiest festival of the Hindu year, celebrated in either October or November. It is known as the festival of light.

**Emigration** The permanent movement of people from one country to another.

**Export** Goods which are sold to or traded with another country.

**Gandhi (Mahatma)** A famous Indian who devoted himself to achieving Independence for India from the British in the 1940s. He led the people in a movement of non-violent protest.

**Green Revolution** In the 1960s many scientific advances were made in farming. Fast growing seeds and chemicals were developed which greatly increased crop production.

**Hinduism** This is one of the oldest religions in the world, dating to beyond 1000 B.C. Hinduism has many Gods. Hindus believe in re-birth or reincarnation.

**Infant deaths** A term used to describe the number of babies who die in the first year of life.

**Irrigation** This is a way of providing water for plants by man-made channels or pipes.

**Jain(ism)** The Jain religion has many similarities with Buddhism. It was founded in the 6th century by Mahvira. Many Jains live in South and South West India. They are strict vegetarians and avoid injury to all living things.

**Muslim** Muslims follow the Islamic religion. This was founded by the prophet Mohammed in the 7th century. Their holy book is called the Koran.

**Paddy field** A small rice field with raised banks around the outsides, called bunds. When heavy rains fall the bunds trap the water inside the field so that it is flooded. Rice begins to grow in the flooded field.

**Plateau** An area of highland with a flat top.

**Produce** A word used to describe crops grown or animals reared by agricultural workers.

**Secular** A secular state is one whose government does not base its laws on the main religion practiced.

**Sikh** The Sikh religion was founded in the 15th century. Sikhs live in the Punjab. The religion is similar to Hinduism but there is no caste system.

**Toddy Tapper** A person who collects the juice from the toddy tree.

**United Nations (UN)** An International organization founded after the Second World War to promote and maintain peace and to help poorer countries to become wealthier.

**Untouchables** Untouchables or Harijans are members of the lowest 'caste-less' group of Hindus. The dirtiest jobs are reserved traditionally for Untouchables. But recently the Government has made it illegal to discriminate against these people.

# Index

## About Oxfam in India

Oxfam works with poor people and their organizations in over 80 countries. Oxfam believes that all people have basic rights: to earn a living, and to have food, shelter, health care and education. Oxfam provides relief in emergencies, and gives long-term support to people struggling to build a better life for themselves and their families.

In India, Oxfam concentrates on helping poor communities to come together, helping people to have more control over their lives and to obtain resources to which they are entitled. As well as providing funds, Oxfam gives advice and training to local groups and helps them to link up and share experience. Particular attention is given to the problems that women face in India. Oxfam is also dealing with environmental problems, such as the effects of drought and the loss of forest land.

The author and publishers would like to thank the following for their help in preparing this book: Joe Human and Lorraine Collett from the Oxfam Asia Desk; Sam Kenrick and the Oxfam Hyderabad office for help in organizing photography; the photographer, R. Lokanadham, of the Centre for Development Communication, Hyderabad; the people of Raipole; the staff of the Oxfam photo library; and the Oxfam Education workers who commented on early drafts.

The Oxfam Education Catalogue lists a range of other resources on economically developing countries, including India, and issues of development. These materials are produced by Oxfam, by other agencies, and by Development Education Centres. For a copy of the catalogue contact Oxfam, 274 Banbury Road, Oxford OX2 7DZ, phone (0865) 311311, or your national Oxfam office.

Photographic acknowledgements
The author and publishers wish to acknowledge, with thanks, the following photographic sources:

*a* = above *b* = below *l* = left *r* = right

Oxfam p29/Oxfam T. Parker pp2, 26; B. Buxton p3; M. Wells pp5, 12; J. Ogle pp6, 10, 11; T. Stack p9; J. Wild p9; S. Safa p13; Centre for Development Communication, Hyderabad/R Lokanadham pp4, 14, 15, 16, 17, 18, 19, 20, 21, 22, 23, 24, 25, 28*r*, 29*r*, Peter Sanders p27; Ben Radford/Allsport p28*l*.

The publishers have made every effort to trace the copyright holders, but if they have inadvertently overlooked any, they will be pleased to make the necessary arrangement at the first opportunity.

Cover photograph © Oxfam/Tricia Parker – Father and child in a village in Rajasthan.

**Note to the reader** - In this book there are some words in the text which are printed in **bold** type. This shows that the word is listed in the glossary on page 30. The glossary gives a brief explanation of words which may be new to you.

First published in Great Britain by Heinemann Library an imprint of Heinemann Publishers (Oxford) Ltd Halley Court, Jordan Hill, Oxford OX2 8EJ

OXFORD LONDON EDINBURGH MADRID ATHENS BOLOGNA PARIS MELBOURNE SYDNEY AUCKLAND SINGAPORE TOKYO IBADAN NAIROBI HARARE GABORONE PORTSMOUTH NH (USA)

© 1994 Heinemann Library

98 97 96 95 94
10 9 8 7 6 5 4 3 2 1

British Library Cataloguing in Publication Data is available from the British Library on request.

ISBN 0 431 07250 7 (Hardback)

ISBN 0 431 07258 2 (Paperback)

Designed and produced by Visual Image
Cover design by Threefold Design

Printed in China